TRANSFORMING
BURNOUT

A SIMPLE GUIDE TO SELF-RENEWAL

ALAN SHELTON, MD

Truly, it is in the darkness that one finds the light,
so when we are in sorrow,
then this light is nearest of all to us.

Meister Eckhart

There are only two ways to live your life.
One is as though nothing is a miracle.
The other is as though everything is a miracle.

Albert Einstein

TRANSFORMING BURNOUT

Copyright © 2007 by Alan Shelton, MD

Published by
Vibrant Press
P.O. Box 8605
Tacoma, WA 98418

FIRST EDITION

Book Design by Jason Oxrieder

Library of Congress Cataloguing-in-Publication Data
Alan Shelton.
Transforming burnout : a simple guide to self-renewal / by
Alan Shelton.
ISBN 0-9787952-0-2
ISBN 978-0-9787952-0-7
1. Self-help 2. Mind and Body
3. Spirituality 4. Health

I. Title: Transforming Burnout. II. Title

1 2 3 4 5 6 7 8 9 10 08 07 06

To Shari, my true companion and richest blessing.

Contents

Foreword

It was an unexpected pleasure and delight to read *Transforming Burnout* by Dr. Alan Shelton. In truth, his story caught me by surprise. Having experienced a severe case of burnout such as Dr. Shelton shares about in these pages, I found that suddenly I was reading that rare self-help book that proves to be directly on point for the reader. Dr. Shelton's open, unguarded style gave me the uncanny experience of "reading excerpts" from my own past, and in this sense reading the book was a truly remarkable "meeting." Not only did I readily identify with the author's experiences and emotions, but also with his sense of wonderment and his questions. In my own case, during the throes of burnout, I had been too afraid to admit my fear and denial. By telling my story and his, which echoes the story of so many others like ourselves, Dr. Shelton has reclaimed the "lost words" we have been unable to speak, fearing criticism or loss of livelihood.

How open certain professionals, especially physicians, will be to applying Dr. Shelton's prescription for transforming burnout—that of reconnection with spirituality—remains to be seen. I sincerely hope that many will find solace in this guidance, just as I have. In his straightforward and gentle approach, Dr. Shelton has managed to bridge a gap that should never have existed in the first place. In actual practice, spirituality and medicine go hand in hand. So many physicians have already begun to recognize this, yet some still remain afraid to admit what a large role our spirituality plays in caring for our patients, and in caring for ourselves.

Dr. Shelton has done a superb job of taking us step by step through the process of recovery from burnout at work—a process he discovered through his own hard-won life experience. While most self-help books only tell you what you *should* do, *Transforming Burnout* offers Dr. Shelton's practical advice and guidance on the specific steps to take to achieve real recovery. Any physician or, for that matter, anyone suffering from the fatigue and despondency associated with burnout at work, will benefit from reading this gem. It is a book that probably will not spend much time on the shelf. It must be shared—with coworkers, professional colleagues, with friends and other loved ones. *Transforming Burnout* provides much-needed insight, delivered by a worthy guide. Dr. Shelton has eloquently articulated the way out of a seemingly unsolvable problem that so many—those in the helping and health professions, as well as those struggling in many other workplaces—have been unsuccessfully striving to give voice to for a very long time. For that, we owe Dr. Alan Shelton our deepest thanks.

David Acosta, M.D.
Clinical Associate Professor, Department of Family Medicine
University of Washington School of Medicine

Acknowledgments

I would like to thank all those who helped me on my journey and supported me in writing this book. I would particularly like to mention Lois Jacobs, my office manager and nurse, who was patient with me and cared for me during my difficult time; Rod Smith, my boss, for his administrative support; and John Vanbuskirk for his friendship and listening ear. I also thank Ted Brackman for helping me clarify my ideas, Holle Plaehn for his encouragement, Andy and Kim Williams for their inspiration, and Ceci Miller for her wisdom and guidance as my editor. A special "thank you" goes to Isadore Tom (Doby) for his healing prayer, and also to the staff and community of the Puyallup Tribal Health Authority for the acceptance and trust they have given to me as their physician. And finally I thank my wife, Shari, and my family for their love and understanding as I pursued this project.

Introduction

This book is the result of my journey through the daunting experience of burning out and coming back to myself again. In the process I not only found a way to recover from burnout, I discovered a much more satisfying way of being at work. After nearly 20 years working as a family practice physician at a Native American community clinic, my burnout problem, which had been brewing for some time, came to a crisis point. I had to get help or I knew I would have to quit the job to which I had been so committed—a job I had once loved doing.

I knew about and had already tried all the usual suggestions for burnout. I took a break, and then another, and then an even longer break from work. But this only added to the amount of work I had to catch up on when I got back! I tried focusing on the parts of the job that I liked the most. These became fewer and fewer until at last there were no longer any parts of the job I enjoyed. I tried sharing my disappointments and struggles with close friends—they quickly tired of hearing me complain. I tried working on a new area of interest, but that only helped for a little while. I tried to get more rest and exercise. At best these various efforts only worked for a short time. I was caught in a seemingly unstoppable downward spiral into despair.

At last I found help from a surprising source—Native American spirituality and the concept of the wellness circle. With these new tools I began rebuilding my feeling of job satisfaction and began again to experience joy in my work. At one point, just to make sure I stayed on task, I scheduled a lecture on burnout with the resident physicians at the hospital where I am a part-time faculty member in the family medicine program. In the talk I presented a case of burnout with which I was extremely familiar—my own. Then I proceeded to describe my recovery using the new approach that was giving me relief and rejuvenating my sense of purpose and enjoyment at work. The talk was surprisingly well received; it had struck a chord with many others like myself. I was invited to give the burnout talk in a number of different venues and was always asked where people could get more information about the approach that was working so well for me. I wrote this book to answer this need, so that those who were interested could learn at a deeper level how to address burnout successfully, how to feel joy in their work, how to feel like themselves again.

Perhaps you started your career feeling idealistic and enthusiastic about what you had to offer, and yet now you feel as though you have nothing left to give. Or you may know a friend or loved one who is suffering from burnout at work. I invite you to take a look at my story, and at the ways in which the wellness circle from the Native American tradition supports me in my work life. I now feel a greater sense of fulfillment than ever before, as I care for patients in our clinic day to day. I am not an expert on burnout, or on Native American spirituality. I am just a man on a journey with a story to tell. It is my hope that by sharing my thoughts and experience here, others suffering from burnout may find relief and greater satisfaction, not only at work but in every area of life.

1

What Is Burnout?

A Case Study (Mine)

Several years ago, after two decades of rewarding but challenging work, I found myself bereft, unable to carry on. I was a family physician practicing in a Native American community clinic when the demands of my work began to overwhelm me. It wasn't sudden, but insidious. A gradual fatigue had crept in, leaving me exhausted and disheartened, scattered and unfocused. All my life I had enjoyed my work and had felt a natural sense of enthusiasm. But now, to my great dismay, that well of energy and inspiration had run dry. I felt drained and used up.

I was burned out.

In bed, I'd hit the snooze button over and over, waiting until the very last minute to drag myself to work. I began to frequently consider that if I got sick, I

wouldn't have to go to work. Thinking this way scared me because I knew it would weaken my immune system and I could truly become ill. What if I had a heart attack . . . or a stroke?

When I finally made it to work I glanced again and again at the clock, looking to escape. The days seemed to get longer and longer. I grew desperate for the weekend. Even though I was seeing many patients, nothing I did seemed worthwhile. I was simply going through the motions. Not only that, I was cranky. I snapped at my staff when things went awry, and as I watched the paperwork pile up on my desk, my despondency grew.

Rather than experiencing the empathy I used to have for difficult or demanding patients, I began to resent them. Their problems now overwhelmed me. What good was I, their doctor, doing them anyway? I grumbled to myself, "They don't exercise, they don't stop smoking, they don't change their diets, but they come back, time and time again, with the same complaints, just wanting more pain medication!" I didn't like the way my mind was changing about people, how my natural sense of compassion had begun to be replaced by stern judgments. I had stopped being the sensitive, caring person I was in the past, the one I wanted to be. Repeatedly I thought, "I just can't do this anymore," and that scared me, too, because I believed I was a good doctor. Practicing medicine was all I had ever wanted to do. But how could I keep going? I had lost the joy that I had always found in my work.

Ever the diagnostician, I considered my symptoms. They sounded a lot like depression and I wondered if that might be my problem. But depressed people have to drag themselves about all the time, I thought, and I had no difficulty getting out of bed on weekends! I still seemed to have plenty of energy to do multiple non-work-related activities. It was puzzling.

I tried taking longer breaks during the day. I took more frequent vacations, during which I would feel fine. But I noticed as soon I returned to the office, I would quickly feel drained again. Not only that but the stack of paperwork hadn't moved, and I groaned under the pressure of so much unfinished business.

For many years I have acted as a clinical faculty member for the family medicine residency at a local hospital. We often discuss particular diseases in a group setting after listening to a case presentation. Mine would have sounded something like this.

Chief Complaint: A 49-year-old white male physician presents to a colleague, "I don't think I can continue to go to work. I have no more energy for it."

History of Present Illness: He has been working in a community clinic for 20 years. He's having a hard time going to work and feels he has nothing left to give. He feels growing resentment toward patients and a minimal sense of accomplishment, and thus has no job satisfaction. This man is despondent about his work and feels as though he is at the end of his rope.

Physical exam and lab are normal and noncontributory.

Differential Diagnosis includes depression, but this is unlikely given his lack of depressive symptoms away from work and on weekends.

The accurate diagnosis? Burnout. My case was a pretty classic depiction of this increasingly common syndrome.

Characteristics of Burnout

Burnout is a common term describing a loss of energy for one's work or profession. It's accompanied by a sense of being used up, of one's vitality being depleted. Burnout has become an especially prevalent stress syndrome among those in the helping or service professions.

Three major symptoms of burnout
Exhaustion
Withdrawal
Loss of job satisfaction

Exhaustion. Burnout is not just physical exhaustion; it is marked by mental and emotional exhaustion as well. A person may feel sad, depressed, and have persistent negative thoughts. He may not be able to come up with creative solutions to even simple problems arising in the natural course of a day. His usual empathy and kindness toward others seems lacking. This aspect of burnout has been called "compassion fatigue." The individual feels drained, used up. It is not that he doesn't want to help or do good work; he simply doesn't feel like he has what it takes to help one more person or to complete one more task.

Withdrawal. The burnout victim shields himself by limiting close involvement with others. He distances himself from clients or patients, becoming cynical, resentful, and less responsive than usual. Defensive, impatient, and easily angered, he withdraws from coworkers.

Loss of Job Satisfaction. The third characteristic of burnout is a direct result of the first two. As things go poorly at work and the person experiencing burnout becomes increasingly ineffective, his sense of personal accomplishment plummets. He realizes he is becoming cold and indifferent, that he's "just not himself," and his sense of fulfillment in work is gone.

Burnout can be quite serious. You can locate burnout in organizations by measuring absenteeism, declining morale, and personal dysfunction. A previously stable and reliable professional may suddenly do something crazy or unexpected. At a recent conference I heard one physician say, "One cool autumn afternoon with all the exam rooms occupied, and with my waiting room full, I quietly slipped out the back door." I knew just what he meant. Even though I had never given in to this impulse when I was suffering from burnout, I vividly remember that powerful desire to escape from work.

Burnout is at the lowest end of a continuum of professional energy. At the high end is the worker's natural sense of enthusiasm and vitality. We all want to be able to approach our work with joy, commitment, and abundant energy, but burnout makes that impossible.

Before reaching burnout there are warning signals: increasing levels of malaise and unhappiness with work.

If we combine all the people who acknowledge this discontent with the ones who have already reached the point of burnout, we have an unacceptably large group of people who experience low morale in their professions, every single day. The struggles, concerns, and frustrations (especially of those in the helping professions) have left many discouraged folks feeling depleted. They rarely experience even the most minimal job satisfaction. They've forgotten what it's like to feel excitement and creativity in their work.

Causes of Burnout

I now regularly give presentations on burnout for people in the health care profession. I usually begin by asking the audience what they believe are the reasons for burnout. Their first guesses are a list of the usual problems and stressful issues faced by people in their field. These run the gamut: difficult or demanding patients, the constant threat of malpractice, unrealistic expectations on the part of their patients or clients, decreasing pay scales, productivity pressure, increasing caseload management tasks, and dealing with difficult psychosocial realities. After a bit of thought, however, it becomes clear that *stress alone does not cause burnout.*

Let's discuss four underlying issues which, along with stress related to one's profession, can lead to burnout. Usually there's a lack of control, a suppression of emotion, a striving for perfection, and a workaholic tendency. We'll look at each of these a bit more closely.

Lack of Control. Those who work in service professions often feel frustrated by the reality of their lack of control over the lives and circumstances of those they seek to help. They may spend a lot of time and effort trying to help someone, only to see that person slip back into choices that created the problem in the first place. For example, J. is an IV heroin user. I treat her secondary problem—perhaps an infection—and address her addiction. She states a desire to quit, so I take extra time to do some counseling, make arrangements, place a few calls, and make plans for follow up (all of this putting me behind schedule). For whatever reason, J. doesn't follow through, and I'm left feeling frustrated, even used. The next time I encounter someone suffering from an addiction, I am less compassionate and even a little cynical. In the helping professions, or in any line of work for that matter, we have to realize that we have very little control over the actions of others.

Suppression of Emotion. Doctors and other health care professionals are taught to be careful in our personal engagement with clients or patients, as this can affect our objectivity. Our feelings, we are taught, might get in the way of proper diagnosis and treatment. Becoming friends with those who seek our help—crying with them over tragedy, rejoicing with them in celebration—all these are frowned upon in traditional medical training. Behaving this way, however, carries a high cost: we tend to lose the ability to be natural and authentic. Relationships outside work that could be supportive and helpful instead turn shallow. We may be experts at being polite, tactful, and evasive, yet we may be unable to express our deepest feelings to those who care about us. Disappointments and frustrations are buried inside, where they grow in secret rather than being expressed, released, and dealt with in a healthy way that allows us to get on with life.

What a difference it would make if we could work with our clients as partners in their health and well-being. As we grew alongside each other, communicating directly and authentically, we could derive a sense of accomplishment from the trials and successes of both our clients and ourselves. And people might be more willing to trust a professional who is more forthcoming with his or her inner state. A pervading sense of trust all around makes everyone more successful and productive at work.

Striving for Perfection. Perfectionism is a double-edged sword. Of course we want to do the best work we can, yet too often those of us who are competent believe that the outcome of our work occurs mainly due to our expertise. Among good doctors, for example, this assumption is great for the ego, but it is arrogant to ignore the multitude of other factors involved in any given treatment situation. In our arrogance we set ourselves up to carry a heavy burden of inadequacy, as not all our patients' health outcomes are as favorable as we would like them to be. We may harbor unresolved guilt when we then, inevitably, make a mistake at work.

Workaholic Tendency. Any job can present potentially unlimited demands on our time and energy. Many people have a hard time setting boundaries and saying *no*. We health care professionals, whose primary work objective is to help people, are particularly susceptible to stretching ourselves beyond our physical limits. The needs are endless, and we get busier and busier. Our resistance to saying *no* when we need to stop can become like an addiction. We may even find that in meeting other people's needs, we ourselves feel affirmed and needed. We become dependent on outside validation as opposed to an inner self-affirmation. For some, a frantic work day provides the rush that makes us feel most alive; hence, the addiction. But at what cost do we pursue this rush? If we don't take the time to meet our own needs, inevitably our personal spring—our inspiration, creativity, and zest for life—runs dry.

There is this fascinating word: *enantiadromia.* (I like to use it to stump my students.) It is a condition in which one's personal identity is bound up with his or her professional identity. When someone asks you who you are, do you respond with your work title? It is quite common for people in my profession to answer, "I'm a family practice physician." But there are many people who, if asked who they are, do not necessarily respond by naming their job. We all have many non-work roles (spouse, parent, friend, golfer, gardener, singer, reader, student, and so forth). For workaholics, or those of us too personally bound up in our profession, these other non-work roles suffer and we lose our balance in life.

A life out of balance leads to burnout. Yet however difficult a person's situation is at work, there is always hope. For someone who chooses to examine his or her life, burnout can become a helpful catalyst, a vehicle of revitalization and renewal, as it was in my case. As I looked at the causes and conditions that had led me into burnout, and as I began to address them, I learned an important truth: that my sense of well-being was not dependent on situations, relationships, or any outer circumstance. My well-being was directly related to the quality of my inner life.

2

What Is Wellness?

About four years ago, my burnout had reached the point of crisis. I became increasingly frustrated and was unable to hide my anger and despair at work. I knew what it was like to be enthusiastic and warm and positive, but I found it impossible to summon up those feelings that had come to me so easily in the past. I became withdrawn and detached from my staff. The nurses and other doctors noticed that I was no longer the same Dr. Shelton they thought they knew. At the time I didn't pay much attention to their reactions, for I was too wrapped up in my own problem. They said very little, actually, but I felt a persistent tension and uneasiness around me at the clinic.

One morning, the psychologist in charge of our mental health branch called me up and said, "Alan, the traditional healer is here today and there has been a cancellation. His name is Doby and he has an opening at noon. Would you be willing to see him?" I was at a loss for words. I stammered a bit, then looked around and asked our charge nurse if we didn't (please!) have a meeting or something at noon. There were no meetings scheduled. Since I couldn't think of a quick excuse, I reluctantly agreed to see the healer. After all, I felt that my psychologist friend wanted me to meet with the healer out of a sense of caring, so I felt some obligation to go along with her suggestion.

I felt awkward, though. I was ashamed to think that others had apparently taken enough note of my condition to conspire to get me treatment, and I did not really expect that the healer would be able to do anything to help me. How would he understand my dilemma when I myself (a doctor!) couldn't even explain what was going on?

I also had some questions and doubts regarding Native American traditional medicine. What was it, exactly? Herbs and ceremony? Was it legitimate? Would it be culturally appropriate for a white guy like me? My hesitancy was complicated by the fact that I was the medical director at a clinical center created to help and treat the Native American community. I wasn't supposed to become one of *their* patients!

With all these conflicting emotions rolling around inside, I made my way to the mental health building and sheepishly entered the traditional healer's room. I was greeted by a short, thick, elderly native man with a white crew cut, dressed in a Pendleton vest and blue jeans. In the corner of the small room sat a middle-aged man with a drum who, I learned later, was Doby's son. He was thin, with a wispy goatee. His long black hair was tied in a ponytail. The hand drum was made of cowhide and had decorative painting on it.

We sat down at a small table in the center of the room. I told him that I was Dr. Shelton. "Oh, yes," he said, looking at his list and smiling. "You are the 'fit in.'" Looking up, he continued, "In order for me to help you, you must believe in spiritual things." I figured he expected a Western medical doctor to be skeptical of his practice, and I assured him that was no problem. I believed in spiritual things, having grown up in a religious family. Even now I still attended church. (I didn't add that this was only when I felt I had nothing better to do.)

"So, what's going on?" he said.

I started with, "Well, it's getting harder and harder for me to come to work."

He put up his hand abruptly, signaling for me to stop. He then began to tell me a story about what had happened around the time of his father's death. To my surprise, the healer didn't want or need to hear any more about my problem. I was a little troubled by this. I had expected that perhaps if he just listened to all the details of my case and asked the right questions, maybe I would leave with a better understanding of what was going on with me. Perhaps things might even improve! I had expected something like a counseling session. I didn't see how this rambling story about his father was going to help. What did his father's death have to do with me?

As I have reflected on this experience over time, it

has occurred to me that traditional healers do not rely on taking a patient's "medical history," as most physicians are trained to do. Rather, they work intuitively. For this reason, Doby didn't need to hear all about my ailment. Now, too, I understand why my more traditional Native American patients were often reluctant to provide the details of their health history. They would say simply, "I am sick." And I would ask, "Well, what is bothering you? Do you have a headache? Cough? Abdominal pain? What is it, exactly?" And they would answer, "I don't know. You're the doctor. You tell me!"

As the healer continued with his story, occasionally his son would interject by chanting a low-pitched, rhythmic *Ooooo* while he beat the drum. This would happen at key points in the story, like when Doby's father told him (on the day before his death) at what time he would die, so that Doby would be sure to be with him. I wasn't sure what to make of this, but assumed it meant that I was to take careful note of the events being described at that moment. I was trying to be a good sport, but I still didn't see how the story, or the chanting for that matter, had anything to do with me.

Finally the healer completed his story and said, "Okay, I'll see what I can do." He got up and came over to me. Placing his hands over my head, he began to sing a native song. His son was drumming, the healer was singing, and I could feel myself moving slightly with the beat. I felt respectful, present, and open, but to be honest, I did not expect anything beneficial to come of this. Doby sang for another five minutes or so, and then he was done.

He announced, "Your spirit had left you, and I put it back." I was astounded. What sort of thing was that to say? My spirit had left and had been put back? I felt no different. I almost laughed, in fact. I wanted to ask him where my spirit had been before he restored it, and struggled to keep my skepticism in check. I didn't want to offend this kind man. After all, he was only trying to help me.

I thanked him and left. What an interesting experience, I thought. Outside the office I said hello to someone I recognized in the waiting room, and then returned to the clinic to begin my afternoon work. As I began seeing patients, my skepticism and amusement quickly turned to marvel. I was back! That was the phrase that came to mind. Once again I felt my old vitality and enthusiasm. I was able to address each patient and problem with the natural sense of compassion and creativity I had known before. When I got double-booked with a difficult patient who was unhappy with the previous treatment of her back pain, instead of getting frustrated I quickly sensed that the real issue was her increased stress, and devised a new plan to her satisfaction. I moved on, feeling pleased with this successful encounter. I had that sort of good energy that we all want—the feeling you have when you know you are at your best. I sensed that I was right in the flow of things. At the end of the day, I was still energized. I felt wonderful!

What had happened? I'm still not sure, exactly, but I suspect that my inner life got "jumpstarted." Unfortunately, over the next few weeks I gradually felt myself drifting back down the continuum of energy toward my original malaise. Once more, I began to feel less energetic and increasingly irritable. I knew I couldn't keep seeing the traditional healer over and over. Anyway, who knew if it would work again? Maybe it had only been a one-shot deal. I needed to find some way to nourish and develop my spirituality. I sensed that if I could discover how to stay spiritually connected and in balance with the whole of life, things would improve again. After much pondering, I became convinced that if I took care of my spirit, my burnout would dissolve.

I began to consider the Native American concept of wellness, which led me to a new approach and a solution to my struggle with burnout. I now have this idea: A well person maintains an enthusiastic commitment to service and has an abundance of positive energy to face challenges. In this way, he or she naturally experiences a fulfilling professional life. Instead of feeling used up and depleted, such a person leaves work each day feeling energized.

So, what does it mean to be *well*? I learned this concept of wellness from people in our Native community, particularly as it is applied in the realm of sobriety and the "good red road." This is the phrase used to describe the lifestyle of close involvement in Native American culture and ceremony that helps one stay alcohol and drug free. I believe this notion of wellness can also be helpful when applied to the issue of burnout.

In the Native American understanding, you are *well* when all aspects of your life are in balance and in harmony. There is a sense of inner peace and wholeness. It is more than the absence of disease, or enjoying good health. The experience of wellness lies beyond whether you are ill or not. You thus might be well while living with a chronic illness. This kind of wellness is reflected in behaviors and attitudes—how you respond to situations, problems, or people.

What does it take for you to lose your cool? Wellness means having a sense of poise and serenity that allows you to respond creatively and responsibly in a crisis. Equanimity and flexibility are natural by-products of true wellness. The higher one's threshold for a "meltdown," the more one is living in a state of true wellness.

How do we improve on our state of wellness? In the Native community where I work every day, I hear constant references to "the wellness circle." The circle is an important sacred symbol for Native Americans. It represents the cycles of life, the four seasons, the four directions, the heavens, Mother Earth, and the universe. It represents a holistic symbol of physical, mental, emotional, and spiritual health in its broadest sense, revealing the parts of human nature that must be nourished to bring a person to wholeness.

Burnout is caused, in part, by living a life out of balance. As I mentioned earlier, someone's identity may be so bound up in their professional existence that the non-work roles in their life fall into neglect. Yet, the idea of balance extends to more than just the various roles in one's life.

The Native American wellness circle describes four aspects or dimensions of life: physical (what one does), mental (what one thinks), emotional (what one feels), and spiritual (what one believes). When all four dimensions of life are in balance and functioning at an optimum level, a person is considered to be physically fit, mentally stimulated, emotionally adjusted, and spiritually connected. To be well, then, means to have vitality in each part of life, and to have all of these parts in relative balance.

Thus, burnout can be addressed from any of these four aspects with the intention of regaining balance. Many of us have learned how to focus on the physical dimension. We are admonished by family, friends, and even our physician to get more rest, do more exercise, have a healthy diet, and avoid harmful habits such as smoking or substance abuse. Or, we might attend to the mental aspect of life by entering cognitive therapy and rethinking some of our approaches and attitudes. Concentrating on the emotional aspect, we could look to relationships for support and perhaps start writing in a journal to better understand our feelings. All of these important and necessary parts of the wellness circle are commonly covered in depth in other resources, such as health and exercise manuals, self-help books, and various therapies.

However, the aspect most neglected—the one most seriously out of balance and in need of recovery in our busy, modern world—is that of the spirit. It is the key component of the wellness circle. Traditionally, the spiritual aspect is considered the foundation or essence of life. I had worked on all of the other areas in my life, yet I still was unable to break out of my burnout until the traditional healer "replaced my spirit." It was at this point that I realized I needed to learn and understand what spirituality was all about. I realized that if I could nourish and develop this area of myself, I could return to a fuller, energetic life, and be truly well.

3

What Is Spirituality?

Spirituality lies beyond the material world of proof, beyond what can be measured or counted. It is made up of the inner life, the realm of belief, mystery, and faith. And yet for all the mystery that surrounds it, spirituality is vital to our well-being. It is the foundation of our most closely held values, the seat of our trust and hope. Spirituality brings purpose and meaning to life, and as we develop it we grow in wisdom and love. We begin to experience a sense of awe, a sense of connection to all of life, and a deep reverence for the Divine. We find ourselves moved to prayers of gratitude and moments of spontaneous worship. Spirituality calls a human being to a life of trust and service.

When our spirituality is nurtured and vibrant, we're "connected." This connection is a sense of relationship to the Creator, Great Spirit, or God (Divine Force), as

well as a relationship to all people and to Mother Earth (our life-giving environment). Spirituality takes us beyond our ego-centered lives by expanding our hearts with compassion toward all.

As a doctor working within the Native American community, I have observed that spirituality forms the framework of many of my patients' orientation to life—it does not dwell in a realm apart. It is not an extracurricular activity. Spirituality involves a reverent attitude toward all things because it awakens us to a divine presence in all things. In this way of seeing and being, all things and persons are interconnected and interdependent. The spiritual world is the unseen world, and thus wrapped in mystery. In the Sioux native language, the word for the Great Spirit is *Wakan*, which means "the great mystery." Yet this spirit, full of mystery, is every bit as real as the visible, tangible world.

It is important to differentiate spirituality from religion. Some people have rejected religion in order to escape what they consider to be oppressive rules and regulations. In the process, however, many lose out on the great gifts of joy and compassion that spirituality brings. Religion and spirituality are related and intertwined, but they are not the same. A person may experience spirituality without being a member of any specific religious affiliation, and even the most "religious" person may feel spiritually bereft.

Spirituality precedes religion. It is that part of human nature which gave birth to religion as an institutionalized system of beliefs, or a creed. The true purpose of religion is to enhance spirituality through ritual and practice. This is accomplished when a person approaches his or her religion as a way to enter the great mystery, to become aware of the sacredness of all life. Religion can become a barrier to spirituality when it insists on narrow, judgmental dogma, and estranges its followers from a sense of connection with the Divine. Religion serves us best as a vehicle to nourish and develop our spirituality. It is possible, however, to get too caught up in the vehicle, the religious practice, while losing sight of the destination, spirituality, which is communion with the Divine and compassion for all.

For modern, academically oriented professionals, like physicians and health care workers, spirituality is often a difficult subject. Our training is framed by science. In Western culture especially, we depend on logical, analytical, and rational approaches, and for good reason. These approaches have successfully ushered in a host of life changing improvements in health care and technology. While honoring science and the mind, however, too often we have come to consider spiritual life as self-indulgent, silly, or even contemptible. Our cultural tendency urges us to devalue belief and mystery, but the result is costly: we're left spiritually starved and out of balance.

As I learned more about spirituality, I began to understand the story told to me by the traditional healer on the day that he held his hand over my head and his son chanted in the corner of the room. At the time, I thought his story had nothing to do with me. Actually, though, the healer was trying to teach me about spirituality. He told me about his father who had also been a traditional healer. Toward the end of his life, the father was making himself ready to enter the spirit world. He wanted to leave his son the knowledge and the gift of healing. For this reason, the father felt it would be important for his son to be present in the moments just before he died. To ensure his son's presence, the father told him what time he would pass on. It happened just as he predicted, and in this way, the son was able to be at his side to receive this gift of healing knowledge.

It is when we are directly confronted with death that we begin to ask life's most difficult questions: the spiritual ones. What is the purpose of life? Where does real meaning come from? What is of real value in our lives? If there truly is a God who loves us, how could there be so much suffering and unfairness in the world? Part of our addiction to the busyness of life is an attempt to prevent ourselves from thinking about the inevitable fact of our own death. But when we keep ourselves too busy to consider the purpose of our existence, our lives cease to have meaning. Strangely, it is only when we fully accept the reality of our mortality that we truly begin to live. This is the point at which we begin to enter into and learn about the spiritual dimension of our humanity.

As French philosopher Pierre Teilhard de Chardin remarked, "We are not physical beings having a spiritual experience, but spiritual beings having a physical experience." Our spirituality is our true essence. It is that part of our life which relates to our soul, which from a spiritual perspective is connected to the Divine and is infinite. This lifetime is but the physical experience of our deeper reality, our spirit, which is our fundamental nature.

At this point, you might ask yourself several questions to help assess your own spirituality. Do I have a sense of connection with the Divine? Do I feel compassion for others? Do I feel awe and reverence, and at the same time a feeling of oneness with the Great Spirit, or God? Do I live a life of trust? Am I called to service? Is prayer or meditation an important part of my life?

You may want to write down your answers and think about them over the next few days (or years). In the next chapter we will explore how you can grow and expand your experience of spirituality. As you do so, the experience of burnout will become a thing of the past.

4

Becoming Spiritually Connected

According to the wellness circle, if we are physically healthy we are considered "fit." Fit for whatever physical task may be required of us. Likewise, if we are spiritually well, we are considered to be "connected," connected both to the Great Spirit (or God) and to the world. We can look at physical fitness as an analogy for spiritual connectedness, and use this as a model to understand, evaluate, and improve the spiritual aspects of our lives.

How do we get fit physically? Most importantly, we must exercise, eat a nutritious diet, and avoid harmful habits such as smoking or substance abuse. Let's look at each of these facets of fitness and consider them in relationship to the spiritual dimension of our lives.

Regular Exercise. In the physical realm, daily exercise or a regular workout is needed to maintain conditioning and fitness. This is particularly true for athletes. If they miss more than a day or two of training, they can expect to fall off in performance. Taking time to pray and meditate each day is the comparable activity in the spiritual realm. Prayer and meditation are the tools you have to commune with your higher power, to help develop and increase your connection to the Divine and to other people. It is no surprise that if we lack a daily discipline of spending time in quiet reflection and gratitude to the Creator, we remain spiritually underdeveloped.

While attending a conference, I once met a Native American elder who had an extraordinary presence that radiated inner strength. He sat quietly and with dignity, and when he spoke everyone listened. Others noticed this about him, and a younger attendee asked him if he was a medicine man. "No," he replied, "but each morning I take time to pray. I welcome the new day by being grateful to the Creator for the gift of life and asking for wisdom and guidance." Early the next morning while heading out for a run, I encountered him sitting quietly in a grassy area under some trees, welcoming the new day with prayer. This man practiced his daily spiritual exercise, and it showed in his wisdom and presence.

For some time now, I have been working on a meditation practice of my own. I call it a *practice* because I keep adjusting it to make it a more personal expression and experience for myself. There is no one right practice for everyone. Each of us needs to develop our own form of prayer and meditation, one that allows us to open ourselves up fully to the Divine. I have a special area in my bedroom near a balcony that offers a view of the north Cascade foothills, and on a clear day, Mount Rainier. Early in the day I pull a rocking chair near the sliding glass door and begin by reading or reciting one of my favorite prayers. One I particularly like is "Lord, Make Me an Instrument of Thy Peace," by Saint Francis of Assisi. This helps set the stage for my day. It puts me into a sacred attitude. Then, because I like to sing, I sing a praise chorus or a special hymn. Most often it is "Spirit of the Living God, Fall Afresh on Me." This music touches me in a deep way each time I sing it, creating an atmosphere where I can be open to spiritual renewal.

I then begin my meditation by sitting relaxed, focusing on my breathing, taking slow and full breaths, letting silence fill my mind. I let go of all the chatter and background worries, trying to quiet all my thoughts to reach this silent, peaceful place. As thoughts come to me, I notice them, then release them by refocusing on my slow, deep breathing. Sometimes I focus on a word, like *peace* or *gratitude*, to still my mind. At other times I picture myself open to and receiving light from above. I enjoy the stillness and try to be receptive, most of all by listening, while I offer my life and invite divine wisdom and love.

I don't have to do this for great lengths of time. I adjust the whole routine according to the time I have available on any given day. Even if I pray and meditate only for a few minutes a day, it brings me an increased sense of well-being and peace. My energy is renewed. In medical research circles this is called the *relaxation response,* which has been shown to have many physical benefits such as lowering blood pressure and decreasing stress hormones. Here, however, I'm talking about the relaxation response in terms of developing one's spiritual self.

Now, there is another key. For this practice to be effective, it has to become a part of one's daily routine. This might be compared to an athlete taking a rejuvenating night's sleep. Here's another example: I have a cell phone which has become an increasingly important tool for my work. I plug it in every night to recharge its battery. On occasions when I forget to do this, I pay a price. In the middle of a conversation, the phone can lose power and my call be disconnected. This concept of daily recharging is an important one in our spiritual lives. We need a daily prayer or meditation practice to keep us spiritually connected and nourished from within.

A Healthy Diet. The second element of being physically fit is eating a healthy diet. What would it mean to feed ourselves a healthy spiritual diet? There is a story of a Cherokee elder talking to his grandson. He tells the youngster that he has two wolves fighting inside himself. One wolf is goodness, love, kindness, joy, and peace. The other wolf is hatred, anger, envy, pride, and greed. The grandson anxiously asks, "Which wolf wins?" The grandfather answers solemnly, "The one that I feed the most." Just as we feed ourselves physically by what we put into our stomachs, we feed our spiritual life by what we put into our minds and hearts.

There are many ways to feed ourselves spiritually. Different things work for different people. A partial list could include participating in religious ceremonies, attending church services, reading inspirational or devotional material, listening to uplifting music, spending time in nature, and helping those who are less fortunate.

Clearly, some of the music we listen to or the material we read feeds the wrong wolf. One of the ways we may feed our spiritual lives with junk food is by watching TV. How often do we sit in front of a TV and zone out, unwittingly letting into our hearts certain things that feed the wrong wolf? Just as we experience negative physical effects from eating a high-sugar, high-fat, high-calorie diet, a poor spiritual diet keeps us spiritually undernourished.

When I have time after my daily meditation, I like to read a few pages from several different books dealing with the inner life, and copy a few words from each in a journal that I keep. This keeps me stimulated and challenged to keep growing and developing, thus effectively nurturing my spiritual diet. (Please look for a list of my favorites at the end of this book.)

Avoiding Bad Habits. Common lifestyle issues or habits that create obstacles to physical fitness include smoking and substance abuse, using alcohol and other drugs. Likewise, there are three particularly harmful habits that block spiritual health and prevent connectedness. These are complaining, holding grudges, and worrying.

Complaining. It turns out that complaining is easy and common. That's the thing about bad habits, they take little effort. Complaining is often our initial reflex when things don't go the way we want them to. People who study these things say that 75 percent of most people's daily conversation is negative.

I was challenged to do an experiment where I would keep track and see how often I complained in a day. This was when I was struggling with burnout, before I had made some changes in my life, including a regular spiritual practice. It seemed like a reasonable thing to do, and feeling up to the challenge, I accepted. The next day I kept track of all my negative reactions and comments, which in fact turned out to be either whining or complaining.

Things started off badly when the alarm rang and, with an expletive, I hit the snooze button. "Uh-oh, that's one!" I thought with chagrin. I got out of bed, went over to the window, and pulled the curtain open. "Oh no, it's another rainy day," I groaned—and just as quickly, "Ah, that's two!" I paused. This wasn't working out so well. I didn't like the idea of having to give such a bad report. Maybe I could recover. After all, there was a lot of day left. "Pull yourself together," I thought. "You can do better than this!" I got in the shower and was beginning to feel pretty good. That great hot water rolled the tension off my shoulders, and then my son flushed the toilet in the downstairs bathroom. "Yikes!" The water suddenly turned cold and I threw a fit. When I finally calmed down, I abandoned the experiment. After all, I had gotten the point. I could now see that I definitely had a problem with negative reactions.

As I thought more about it, I came to the realization that with every complaint there is also an opportunity to be grateful. All I would need to do was simply look at the situation from a different perspective. For example when the alarm rang, I could have been grateful to wake up to a new day. With the abundant rain, I could feel grateful to live in a part of the country where there is so much lush green vegetation. And as for the shower going cold, I could be thankful that my son had gotten out of bed and was busy getting ready for his day.

Actually, being grateful is the opposite of complaining. It turns out that gratitude is an important part of spirituality. It is difficult to be open to divine will or inner guidance when we are frequently complaining. On the other hand, when we are grateful, we enter a place of increasing peace and joy. Gratitude changes how we experience life. It turns our so-called ordinary experiences into blessings. Being grateful, even when times are difficult, changes our perspective to one of trust. Trust and complaint cannot coexist. The habit of complaining blocks spiritual connectedness, just as the habit of gratitude and trust opens the doorway to spiritual peace.

I developed a new habit of keeping a gratitude journal to help change my habit of complaining. (I have my wife to thank for this, as she purchased me one for my birthday. I wonder why!) Each night when I go to bed, I write down the things that happened during the day which I am thankful for or which I recognize as being special blessings. I have found that what I focus on grows. As I focus on seeing things in a positive way, I perceive that my life is abundantly blessed, every day.

Holding a grudge. This second habit is also easy and common. Refusing to forgive, carrying resentment, and being critical of others—all of these are traps. We have all been hurt, and our memories tend to be long. It is easy to judge someone whom we think has wronged us. We don't want to let go of that chip on our shoulder. Unfortunately, the resulting bitterness poisons the spirit and closes the heart. Unresolved anger and hostility can destroy one from the inside. In my work as a physician, I often hear patients complain of somatic pain (pain without clear evidence of cause). When these patients share what's going on in their lives, they often reveal an ongoing resentment toward a parent who neglected or didn't love them, or a spouse who betrayed them. In such cases, holding a grudge clearly takes a toll on physical health.

Forgiveness, on the other hand, can be joyful and freeing, while also bringing great peace of mind. Forgiveness isn't something we do for the one who wronged us; we do it for ourselves. Forgiveness is the process of letting go of the past and beginning to trust again. Doing this opens the heart and allows new and better experiences to enter in.

Sometimes, however, forgiveness is especially difficult. In such cases it is helpful to remember that those who harmed us in the past were often reacting from within the prison of their own limited ways of being. For this reason, the bad behavior of others rarely has anything to do with us. As we understand our past hurts in this way, we move toward a greater understanding of our connection to the rest of the living world, in all its divinely created pieces, of which we are a part.

It is just as important to learn to forgive ourselves for our perceived failures or inadequacies. As we let go of judging others and forgive instead, self-judgment becomes less likely. While holding a grudge blocks spiritual connectedness, forgiveness builds and nourishes it. By forgiving, we open ourselves up to understanding and compassion toward those who have hurt us. And by doing this, we foster trust in the Divine and begin to open ourselves to its sacred work in our lives.

Worry. The third habit that blocks spiritual connectedness is worry. Often we carry a core of anxiety, a tightness or tension that causes us to want to get away and relax. Anxiety is a major modern malady, a symptom of our hectic, busy lives. One of the most common diagnoses at our clinic is anxiety, and for this reason, one of the most common drugs dispensed is Xanax, a type of tranquilizer medication. Unfortunately, it has the characteristic of producing both tolerance and dependence, meaning that with time, one requires increasing amounts of the drug to get the same effect (tolerance), and that without the medication, one feels one's symptoms more intensely than before (dependence).

Anxiety is common in health care providers. They are often concerned about whether they have missed a diagnosis. They worry about the outcome of treatment for their sick patients. The opposite of worrying, of course, is peace of mind. And to experience peace of mind, we must be aware of our inner life, the life of our spiritual self.

A few years ago I was talking with a patient who was 100 years old. His mind was pretty clear and he still lived independently. I found this remarkable, so I asked,

"What's your secret?" He said, "Well, I have always tried to get plenty of activity, but I think, more importantly, I just don't worry a whole lot about anything." His answer confirmed that releasing worries may be even more important for health and longevity than I had previously realized.

When we worry, we release biochemicals into our bloodstream that produce stress and increase blood pressure, starting a whole cascade of reactions called the fight-or-flight response. This is a perfectly useful protective mechanism that comes in quite handy if we are hunting a tiger in the jungle. In our modern society, however, this stress response can create illness.

How do we change paths from worry and anxiety to peace of mind? Much spiritual literature concerns itself with mindfulness, or being wholly in the moment. Clearly, most worries and anxieties are about things that have already happened which we stew about afterward, or about something we fear might happen in the future. The habit of being present in the moment, as opposed to worrying about some other time—the past or the future—is the key to this state of mindfulness.

Thich Nhat Hanh, a Zen Buddhist monk, teaches a great exercise on mindfulness and peace that goes something like this: While breathing in, think of calmness and tranquility. While breathing out, smile. (It is amazing what the physical act of smiling can do for one's emotional state.) Think about the present moment on the next inward breath. Then, breathing out, declare to yourself that this is a wonderful moment! This simple practice is a remarkable tool for moving from a worried state to a place of calmness.

Another approach to moving from anxiety to peace of mind is through the use of prayer. In prayer we turn over our fears and worries to a power greater than ourselves: God, or the Divine Presence, or the Peace of the Universe. This brings a new spiritual perspective into our life experiences, reminding us that there is a greater reality beyond our limited viewpoint. Ultimately, prayer brings us into a state of trust. We trust that we are in the hands of the Divine, and that in the end, all will be well.

So we have seen that the habits of complaining, holding a grudge, and worry prevent or limit spiritual growth. It is also true that their opposites—gratitude, forgiveness, and peace of mind—nourish and promote our spiritual lives and can help prevent us from burning out.

5

The Impact of Spirituality on Work

A healthy spirituality leads to overall wellness. For this reason, it is bound to have a powerful impact on your life at work. You can look at the impact of your spirituality on your work in four significant ways: your calling, your attitude, your expectations, and your need for control.

Calling Think about how you came to your present situation. Did it happen by chance, by luck, or was it the result of careful preparation? For most of us, somewhere along the way, things (usually beyond our control) simply fell into place. When I applied for my medical residency training, a computer system matched my ranking of residency programs to their ranking of senior medical student applicants. I felt a little helpless just filling out

some form and then waiting for a computer to decide where I was going to spend an important part of my life.

Before I found my current clinical job, I went to an Indian Health Service meeting where I was told that they had no openings in Washington State. But at the same meeting, by chance, I met someone who informed me about a tribally run clinic, not managed by the IHS, that was looking for a physician in a nearby city. Coincidence? Possibly. I took the job expecting that I would stay there for about two years and then move on. Twenty-two years later I still work there, seeing patients, making friends, living life, and doing the work I have always felt called to do.

From a spiritual perspective, each one of us has been led or called to our current position. Accepting this concept can have profound implications. The belief that the Great Spirit, or the Divine, guided you to your present work gives it more meaning. Knowing this, you understand that you have been chosen for your work because of your unique set of gifts or abilities to meet specific needs. The true purpose of your gifts and the needs they meet may even be beyond your knowledge. It may also be that some aspect of your work may meet a specific need of your own. Not only do you have something to share, but you also have something to receive or learn.

In any case, such a belief gives you energy and resolve when times are difficult or overwhelming. It expands your comprehension and dedication as it opens the possibility that your work is sacred. There is now this divine element of an overriding plan that gives purpose and meaning. You are not where you are by accident. You have a sense of calling.

Attitude. How would a healthy spirituality affect your attitude? Attitude is a reflection of self, what you feel and think. It's how you approach life. At Stanford University a study was done on peak performance. The researchers found that the most important factor in peak performance was attitude. It was more important than intelligence, talent, education, or luck. The researchers actually calculated a figure to represent the importance of attitude. They found that the quality of our lives and our potential for thriving are 80 percent attitude and 15 percent ability.

The amazing thing about attitude is that we choose it. Some have said that this is the greatest freedom we have as human beings. No matter what happens, we have the ability to interpret that event. We can interpret an event in a negative way and choose a bad attitude, or we can interpret an event in a positive way and choose a good attitude. Even difficult or problematic situations can be seen as a chance for character growth, or as something forcing us to rely on the inner life and develop character in that way.

Clearly our attitudes can be impacted by spirituality. If we enter each day with a sense of reverence toward all, if we are open to the Divine and come to all problems with trust, we will respond with expectancy. Instead of being defensive and struggling with frustration in the face of inevitable problems, we can have a hopeful, open response. When we're operating out of that mind-set, we're at our most creative and most able to solve problems successfully.

Every day I have a choice of reactions when my beeper goes off. The beeper doesn't always go off when it's convenient, so when I hear the beep, am I annoyed? Frustrated? Upset or anxious? Thich Nhat Hanh also teaches a simple spiritual practice for dealing with situations that often elicit negative reactions. It works like this: When the beeper goes off, take a deep slow breath, and smile. (As we've seen, it is amazing how smiling affects your emotions.) Then say to yourself, "This is a wonderful opportunity to use the knowledge that I have been given to help someone else." This practice has had a profound effect on my experience of being paged on my beeper.

I now try to incorporate this practice into my patient encounters. Before I enter the room, I pick up the chart and pause for a moment, taking a deep, slow breath. I try to let go of all the other things that are happening around me, the call from the hospital regarding the patient in labor, the patient in the urgent care room who is having an asthmatic attack, the demanding patient still yet to be seen, and so on. There are many things that might distract me from the present moment. As I put these things aside, I invite the Creator, the Great Spirit, to be with me and to be part of my encounter with the patient I am seeing right at this moment. I ask the Divine to love the patient through me. As you might imagine, remembering to do this makes a big difference!

The other day, I entered the room after saying this prayer and encountered a sullen, angry young woman who said, "I don't know why I come here. You people do nothing for me. I still have my headache!" She was quite angry. If I had not prepared myself in advance with a prayer, I might not have been in the right frame of mind to hear her comment. Approaching her with a negative attitude, I might have responded abruptly and defensively, something like, "Well I can tell by your chart that we have done many things, including ordering these tests and trying several medications." But because of my prayer, I was not in a confrontational mood. I had an open, loving attitude. I was able to say to her, "I'm sorry that you don't feel better. Let me start over. Give us another chance. Please tell me again about your problem and we'll see if we can come up with a better plan." Her anger melted away immediately, perhaps because I responded in kindness and she felt heard and valued. The visit quickly became a productive, healing encounter instead of a frustrating confrontation.

An encounter like this brings great hope and an even deeper commitment to nurture my spiritual life. It is difficult for me to make a practice of choosing a positive attitude each day, however, if I do not continue to nourish my spirituality. A healthy spiritual connection is no accident. It can definitely foster and encourage happiness and a positive attitude, but only if I keep it going!

Expectations. A third area where spirituality has a great impact is on our expectations. I'm quite susceptible to high expectations. Physicians tend to be perfectionists. Consequently, we have fierce expectations of ourselves and others. As noted earlier, this can be one setup for burnout. When we have high expectations and these expectations are not met, it can create fertile ground for feeling disillusionment and discouragement.

There seems to be this one-in-ten tipping point. If one out of ten things doesn't go quite right, the other nine that went okay pale in significance. We can carry that one disappointment around with us, even to the extent of bringing sour attitudes home to our loved ones.

A similar idea is expressed by the following formula: E ± R = S. The E is expectation, the R is reality, and the S is stress. Expectation plus or minus Reality equals Stress. In other words, the difference between what you expect to happen and what really happens is the amount of stress you will have to deal with. This emphasizes why high expectations can become a trap.

From a spiritual perspective, expectations must be offered up and released to divine will. We have hope, we intend and want good results, but we must let go of attachment to specific expectations and outcomes. Therefore if we want to be spiritually well, we must cultivate trust, the belief that whatever the outcome, it is in the hands of the Great Spirit or the Divine. This is a movement away from holding on to expectations, to a position of openness, where our value, worth, and happiness is not tied to any particular outcome. Through this spiritual perspective, we let go of any unmet expectations that might drag us down.

At one time, we had a physician working at our clinic whose expectation was that before he saw any patient he would have their chart in hand to review. Now in general, this is a good expectation. In fact, this was our clinic's policy. There are a lot of good reasons to have a patient's chart in hand before and during the visit, including a much better chance of delivering quality care. The problem is that we run a busy outpatient clinic and there are a lot of places where a patient's chart may end up. It's not always easy to track them down. On one occasion, it came to my attention that this doctor was in his office with a grim expression on his face, the patient was upset about having been kept waiting for an hour, and the nurses were beside themselves unable to locate the needed chart. What's wrong with this picture? We had lost sight of our essential mission—to take care of people's health. I gently explained to the doctor that in this case, it just might be that he was meant to see the patient without the chart. Since then, I have come to look at such situations with the attitude that sometimes the patient's visit is more fruitful when he or she is seen by a doctor unbiased by the notes or history appearing on the chart.

When I first began practicing medicine, I had the expectation that all my patients, whatever ailment they might present, would get better upon treatment. Logically, it followed that they would then appreciate and like me. How naïve this seems to me today. Once I abandoned this expectation, I experienced a fresh new sense of freedom. Fortunately, even though I no longer carry this expectation, I am richly blessed with the love and appreciation of the community that I serve.

Control. The issue of control is closely related to that of expectation. Our spirituality can have a significant impact on how we relate to issues of control. We often struggle to have more control. Indeed, we fight against losing control in most areas of our lives. We want to control our children, our spouses, our clients, our co-workers. But this desire to maintain control often leads to frustration. At the heart of spirit is mystery. The need for control, however, stifles mystery and blinds us to its wonders. When we are spiritually well-adjusted, we do not allow ourselves to be bothered by things over which we have no control. This is a truth we can practice accepting every day. Ultimately, we have very little control over anything in our lives other than our attitude or our interpretation of events. The spiritual response to issues over which we have little control is *trust*. This powerful shift in perspective requires a release of our "should be's" in favor of an acceptance of divine will.

A number of years ago at our organization, we found a way to fund the hiring of a new physician. I was excited about the possibility of hiring another family practice doctor who could help with on-call duties and hospital rounds. This doctor would be required to deliver infants and to take care of children, adults, and elders. During this time of planning, I got word from the board of directors, the tribal council, that we were to hire a pediatrician. They felt that it was important to have a child-care specialist on staff.

A pediatrician! This was not, in my opinion, the direction in which we should proceed. A family doctor could take care of children, as well as tend to all the other issues we needed to address. Surely they were mistaken! Clearly we needed someone else who could take calls and deliver babies. "What does the tribal council know about health care anyway?" I thought. "They are just popularly elected officials." I steamed and stewed like this for a few days. In the end, it became clear that the board was in charge. This was their clinic, and they wanted a pediatrician not a family practice physician. After several meetings with our administrative staff, we proceeded to hire a pediatrician. Looking back now, I realize that it was one of the best new ventures ever undertaken by our health organization.

We now have a strong pediatric department that works within the community to promote health in children and young people. It turned out to be a good thing that I didn't have the control I would have liked over this decision. In such cases, it's quite possible that a wisdom beyond ourselves is operating, working things out for the greater benefit. A healthy spirituality helps us let go of our sometimes short-sighted personal attachments, and leads to faith in a greater intelligence. In this way, we begin to trust in reality as it is, even when we're not immediately able to see the benefit.

As I accept my calling in life, as I practice a positive attitude, as I trust and let go of expectations and my need for control, my inner life brings greater and greater peace and happiness—regardless of whether I get what I want. This not only prevents burnout on the job, but it also brings fulfillment and satisfaction in the present moment.

6

Trust

In each of the issues discussed earlier—sense of calling, attitude, expectations, and control—the operative word for being spiritually connected is *trust*. This type of trust is a belief that cannot be seen or proved, a belief that our ultimate identity is spiritual, and a belief in the love in which the Divine holds us all.

Joan Borysenko, a PhD from Harvard and past instructor in mind/body medicine at the Harvard Medical School, expounds on a psychology of spiritual optimism in her book *Fire in the Soul,* in which she states that everything that happens to us, all negative and positive experiences, are actions of grace in the service of Love, meant to move us to a place of greater freedom and happiness.

In difficult situations (such as divorce, death of a

loved one, some life tragedy, or even burnout at work), we come to a certain place. It is in this place that we face our most closely held beliefs. This is a place full of possibility as well as pain, and therefore it is sacred. It is also somewhat dangerous because in this place we can decide to respond to our difficult situation in one of two different ways. We can react with fear, guilt, and bitterness, blaming ourselves and others. Or, when we come to this place, we can respond with optimistic spiritual hope and trust, accepting the difficult situation as an opportunity to learn and grow.

Albert Einstein was once asked what he thought was the most important question that each person needed to answer. He replied: "Is the universe friendly or not?" Indeed, this question is crucial. To believe in a divine force that acts in love toward us is to take a spiritual perspective, and to live with faith and trust. The alternative to this perspective is fear. Trust comes from our highest Self and connects us to a greater whole, giving us a new perspective beyond what we can know or observe with our physical senses. Fear keeps us trapped and limited by self-doubt.

Looking back on my time of despair in the midst of burnout, I now see it as a gift. Although it was a painful and difficult time, being burned out forced me to take a new and broader look at my life, resulting in an opportunity to deepen and strengthen my spiritual understanding. Because of my burnout, I'm learning to be open to the possibilities of each day, letting go of control and replacing it with trust that a higher power is leading and guiding me.

I have a patient who suffered a horrible accident as a child, which left him disfigured and disabled. In his youth he found solace in alcohol and drugs. Now as an adult he is sober and living in recovery, after reconnecting with his native spirituality. If anyone has a right to be angry and bitter, this man certainly does. But on the contrary, he is always pleasant and friendly, looking for the positive in every situation. Recently, he told me that he wants to work with young people to encourage them in their efforts to avoid alcohol and drugs. In spite of his tragedy, or perhaps because of it, he has found great purpose and meaning in his life, through a determination and commitment to help others.

I have another patient who suffers from chronic pain, depression, and anxiety. Although she takes many medications, she barely copes and is filled with bitterness and anger. One day she shared with me how she hates God because of a car crash long ago, in which some children she loved were badly injured, and some died. I realized with a start that she was referring to the very same accident that my other patient had survived. Sadly, this woman has not yet found her way to faith and trust, and lives a life so racked with resentment that little room is left for peace and enjoyment, much less the fulfillment that might come from contributing to the lives of others.

Recently, my good friends Andy and Kim Williams have been going through the very difficult kind of crisis that every parent fears. Their 15-year-old son Caleb, a gifted basketball player, suffered a tragic accident. While saving a friend who got in trouble climbing a rope swing, he lost his own balance and fell 20 feet onto the rocks below, and then into the Snoqualmie River. Through the heroic efforts of some classmates who were also swimming that day, his head was held above water for 45 minutes until the emergency crew was able to reach him. Caleb was flown by helicopter to Harborview Hospital, where he was treated for a severe brain injury and several fractures. He lay comatose for several months before a gradual recovery and grueling rehabilitation process began.

Caleb's parents, family, and friends endured much uncertainty in those first days of shock and anguish. Would he live? Would he be disabled? Would he ever be able to return to school or play basketball again? The days were filled with hugs, tears, and countless prayers.

I was present with Andy and Kim on several occasions while they talked with Caleb's physicians. One day my friends were told that even if their son recovered from his comatose state, he would most likely never be the same. They brought Caleb home to the hospital bed they had set up in their living room, not knowing if he would ever wake up, not knowing how long they would be able to care for him by themselves. These were deeply trying times for Andy and Kim.

And yet somehow they persisted in focusing on the positives. Caleb's brain injury wasn't fatal. There didn't seem to be any spinal cord injury or paralysis. Their kind-hearted son had probably saved another's life. Among the church and school friends who gathered to help, a deep sense of community grew. Many of the young people who got involved in helping to care for

Caleb experienced dramatic growth in their own spiritual lives. Still, the daily struggle and uncertainty and the frequent feelings of helplessness made this one of the most challenging situations Andy and Kim—and their community—had ever faced.

One day I commented to Kim about the courage and poise she had shown in the face of such hardship. She was such a trouper, hanging in there with Caleb daily in the hospital, learning to administer his medicines and do the tube feedings at home. She told me that God gave her strength day by day. She also admitted that at times the grief and fear were overwhelming. On one particular day, Kim shared, as she drove to the hospital she felt a deep despair. She prayed that God would help her accept whatever happened. It seemed to be a turning point for Kim, as she felt a new sense of peace. Each day now, she renews her trust that God has a bigger plan for Caleb's life. The story is not finished, after all. Kim believes there is a purpose greater than anything that they could have planned or imagined, and that keeps her going.

Two months after the accident, we got the exciting news. Caleb was waking up! It was a wonderful moment when I went to visit and Caleb met me at the door. Family and friends were thrilled and overjoyed. It was such a relief that he could walk and talk again. He has continued to make progress, and with hard work in rehab, he is now back in school.

As his doctors predicted, however, Caleb's memory, speech, and motor skills are not the same. It doesn't appear likely that he will ever play basketball again. For

Andy, this realization has been deeply disappointing. He had coached Caleb on select basketball teams and had watched him develop into a promising player. Recently he said, "I had dreams for him. He was such an unselfish player who made the other players do better. He had a great attitude. For Caleb, it was always about the team. Sometimes I got angry and lost hope that anything positive could ever come of this. I would ask myself, 'Why did this have to happen to such a good kid?'"

Then Andy shared that at one point, Caleb had a high fever which lasted all night. Andy felt immobilized by fear and helplessness. "My comfort zone was always in trying to control things. I felt so scared because I had absolutely no control. I just reached the end, and I had to let go. At that moment I gave up Caleb, his life, his future, and my dreams for him to God."

Now Andy is in a different place. He's more open and accepting. He says he sees life in a more "heavenly" way. As a result of Caleb's challenges, Andy now realizes more deeply how short life is. Because he believes that reality consists of more than this physical lifetime, Andy now focuses on serving others, remembering that there is always someone less fortunate than he.

My friends' story is still unfolding, but their son Caleb has already had an inspirational impact on the community that no one could have anticipated. Recently there was an article in the local newspaper about how the Mount Si basketball team is having an unforgettable season playing for Caleb, their teammate, who now cheers them on from the stands. The team won their league, and went on to the Washington State tournament for the first time in nearly 30 years. The players say that Caleb has given them extra motivation and inspiration. Their perspective has changed; now they take nothing for granted. There are also the gifts of living with a deeper focus, of working and playing for the sake of something greater than themselves and their personal desires.

Andy and Kim inspire me again and again, as I watch their example of persistent trust in the face of a situation that could have dashed their hopes. By trusting that a divine (if mysterious) purpose is the true underpinning of their difficulties, they have found meaning in the midst of suffering and loss.

Trust allows us to enter into a spiritually focused life, one in which we accept that our essence is spiritual and that this essence cannot be harmed or damaged. Trust leads us to the certainty that there is a greater purpose and meaning in the events of our lives, a purpose that goes beyond a limited, individual viewpoint. With trust we come to the delightful realization that no matter what happens we are not alone, we are loved by the Divine in a wondrous way.

Trust gives us energy when our lives don't go according to our personal plans. Trust in a divine purpose gives us strength when circumstances seem to stretch us past the breaking point. If burnout is the state of burning up all the reserves we had and then some, a spiritually focused life is the fuel that gives us endless reserves of courage, and the wisdom and will to stand firm, no matter what.

7

The Gifts of Spirituality

On my path of recovery from burnout, spirituality has brought me many gifts. I especially want to mention these three: purpose, presence, and power.

Purpose. Working on my inner life, I have found a renewed sense of purpose. When I first went into medicine, I was young and idealistic. I wanted to work and serve in a community where I was needed. I wanted to make a difference in people's lives. Originally, I came to the clinic on the reservation because it seemed like they needed me and I could make a difference there. The community had been pushed to the margin of society and was struggling with many issues related to poverty. In spite of all of this, the people had a vitality, spirit, and vision that intrigued me. I wanted to help and to be a part of the effort to improve their health care.

Eventually, my burnout cost me. It took away my

enthusiasm, my dedication, and my sense of purpose. My energy had dwindled to the point where my goal was simply to make it through the day. Work was survival. There was nothing expansive, caring, or creative about it.

Now, however, I begin my day with the spiritual practices of meditation and prayer. As I take this time, I come to a place far beyond the simple, idealistic desire to help bring health to a community (as good as that sounds). As my spirit grows, I am able to see each patient as more than a physical being with some health issue, chronic disease, or addiction. I see each person as having a true Self, an essence that is spiritual. I try to connect with each one in a deeper way, hoping to share light and blessings. As I attend to their health issues, I try also to encourage my patients to become who they truly are.

Approaching my work this way actually expands the gift of my purpose to include the gift of compassion, as well. Compassion allows me to see others as more than their outer appearance. When I look at another with compassion, I see beyond the burden of their misery. Instead I recognize their essential goodness, even if it is buried deeply inside. Seeing the beauty of the souls of my patients, I can act with blessing and love toward them. Once again let me remind you of the key: I am only able to do this as long as I continue to regularly engage in my own practice of meditation and prayer. My spiritual practice pushes me to this higher sense of purpose, which in turn fills me with a sense of worth and usefulness.

My wife, who teaches art and creative writing at a nearby middle school, has a wonderful way of welcoming each student as he or she enters the classroom. In

India it is common to greet others with a bow and the word *Namaste*, which means "The divine within me sees and greets the divine within you." As she does this, my wife blesses the students and wishes them well as they enter her room. She says that this is one tool she uses to remind herself each day of how precious each child is. I try to greet my patients with the same love and grace. Practicing compassion in this way, spirituality brings an enhanced sense of purpose.

Presence. A second gift of spirituality is the sense of presence that it brings. I've experienced this blessing in two ways. First, I have begun to feel the presence of the Great Spirit. There is a joyful confidence, a peaceful quality about this presence. I pause during my day, take a breath, and say a prayer inviting the Divine to bless and inspire my next meeting with a patient. Often, something new and dramatic occurs. As I create space for a spiritual presence to enter, my attitude changes. I become less judgmental, less defensive, and more accepting. My gift for coming up with creative solutions is at its peak. I am intuitively connected to my patient. Without this connection to the Divine, I would have no room for this perspective.

In the past I might have said a prayer asking God to help me with some endeavor or task, but just saying the words didn't reshape my attitude. Back then, I was not aligning myself with divine will. Instead, I had expectations that God would grant me favors. I had an agenda that I wanted God to fulfill, and when that didn't happen, I became resigned and discouraged. Now, by opening myself up to listening instead of telling, the answers I need often come almost instantaneously.

The second gift of presence is that of my own true Self. In the past, as a busy, enthusiastic doctor, I prided myself on my ability to multi-task. I was trying to do everything so efficiently that I ended up in a frenzy. I would often do several things at once, such as writing patients' charts while I ate my lunch. Not surprisingly, I ended up stressed and anxious.

Now I am learning to practice moment-to-moment awareness. It's about paying full attention to the present moment. It used to be so easy for me to get distracted by thoughts and emotions, which would take me far away from the reality directly in front of me. I was lost in my own head, reacting to the patient through the filters of my thoughts and reactions. Now when I feel myself drifting away from the present, I stop for a moment to get quiet, take a deep breath, and let go of all distractions. Doing this throughout the day, I can fully attend to each task and each person I meet.

When I enter an exam room to see a patient, I don't want to be thinking about the previous patient or about what's happening over at the hospital or about some dispute between two coworkers. I want to relate with integrity to each person I meet. By practicing meditation, I have learned to hold my thoughts in awareness without letting them take over. I can see those distracting thoughts as "just thoughts," not reality, and this allows me to release them. If I notice anxiety, which has no problem-solving function, I can view it as a simple reaction and quietly brush it away. Doing this, I can attend to the next task with full attention.

At first glance it may seem like I am taking more time than necessary as I meet with people. But in fact, the saying "haste makes waste" is true. By being fully present, I have become a much more efficient doctor: the task gets done the right way the first time. I get to the heart of the matter more effectively. This reduces the feeling of struggle, so that I have more joy in everything I'm doing.

Power. The last gift is that of power. This is not the kind of power people ordinarily think of—it is not authority, control, or influence. In fact, it may seem like the opposite. The spiritual gift of power is the strength to trust and let go. Spiritual power means trusting God, yourself, your intuition, and your capacity to do well, and trusting the other people you meet. Spiritual power means letting go of anxiety, fear, worry, resentment, frustration, and even fatigue. It is rightly called *power* because letting go of the need for control, of expectations, of agendas, and of inner turmoil is not easily done.

In graduate school years ago, I was involved in a leadership training workshop with some highly motivated and accomplished peers. It was a little intimidating. During one session, we were asked to share our highest achievement at that point in our lives. There were a few past university valedictorians, student body presidents, prestigious scholarship recipients, some state champion athletes, and a variety of other honors and awards were mentioned. I began feeling better; I had a few of these credentials myself. Then one of the last members of the group spoke. He said that his greatest achievement to date was when he had been able to surrender his life—his goals and ambitions—to God. The room got very quiet. I'm not sure that any of us knew what this man was talking about. But I've thought about what he said on occasion, and his words have become more significant to me lately.

Why is this surrender such a great achievement? Why does letting go result in power? Because, put simply, letting go is hard to do. We don't naturally want to let go of things that seem important to us, such as the perception that we have control over our lives, our loved ones, or our work. As we develop in spiritual life, however, we gain new perspective. We come to realize that our ultimate life is in the spirit. This realization allows us to begin releasing our attachments to external life: to our appearance, the kind of car we drive, how much money we earn, our position on the social ladder, and so on. As our sense of spirituality develops, we experience a reverence for our lives and for the lives of others. We see the delicate weavings of a master plan, and this gives us the gift of being able to release our attachments and turn them over to a higher power, to the Creator of the master plan.

Part of the power to trust or let go comes from the further realization that from our position as the created and not the Creator, we don't have the wisdom to perceive the ultimate good that may be present in any given situation. In the sweat lodge ceremony, my Native friends refer to human beings as "the pitiful two-legged." From our limited viewpoint, how could we know what is truly in our best interest?

Recently, I heard someone share a great story. A farmer in China bought his son a horse on his eighteenth birthday. "Oh, that is very good fortune," said the neighbors. But the farmer was wise and only said, "We'll see." Sure enough, tragedy struck: the boy was thrown while riding the horse and broke his leg. "Oh, this is very bad fortune," said the neighbors. Again the farmer answered, "We'll see." The next month the emperor's troops swept through town and conscripted all the young men, taking them off to fight a faraway war. As the sorrowing families watched their sons riding away, possibly never to return, they noticed the farmer's injured son alongside them, also waving goodbye to the other boys. The army had no use for him. Perhaps his broken leg had been good fortune after all! As the story shows, we often spend a lot of energy worrying if things don't work out as we planned, when instead we could put our trust in divine wisdom. Spiritual power comes from letting go of our need to control, releasing expectations of how things should turn out, and trusting in the Divine.

Spirituality offers us many gifts. The gifts I have mentioned here are just the beginning! Along with the gift of purpose, for example, comes a sense of calling and compassion. With the gift of presence comes a peaceful attitude and authentic joy. With the gift of the power to trust comes wisdom. Now that I have begun to receive these gifts, I consider my burnout to have been a blessing. It forced me to reexamine my spiritual life and commit to working on it as a lifelong discipline.

8

Final Blessings:
Four Pearls

Make me a channel of your peace.
Where there is hatred, let me bring your love,
Where there is illness, your healing power,
Where there is sorrow, joy forever more . . .

O Spirit, grant that I may never seek
So much to be consoled as to console,
To be understood as to understand,
To be loved as to love with my whole soul!

Make me a channel of your peace . . .

Saint Francis of Assisi

Remember what a desperate state I was in when I began this journey? I had lost my commitment to a job I once loved. I was angry at my patients for their demands on me. I felt like a walking fraud, barely making it through each day. I was irritable and demanding of my staff. All I could think of was to give up and quit.

Then one kind person did a simple act of service for me. She sent me to a spiritual healer. And gradually, over time, I rebuilt my life into something new. Can you believe me when I say that it is possible to go from cynicism and crushing weariness to joy—just by shifting your perspective? And yet that is precisely what happened for me. Joy is the gift spirituality has brought into my life.

I have always liked the idea of a "bottom line" to any problem or issue, a take-home message that wraps it all up in a concise statement easily remembered. In the residency program where I teach we call these "pearls," little summations of the major points at the end of a talk or presentation. So as I sit in my special place contemplating my journey out of burnout into blessing, what are the pearls? What are those nuggets of wisdom that I learned and hope to share?

The First Pearl. The value of spiritual wellness is pan-cultural. Every tradition points to its importance. In *The Little Prince* by French author Antoine de Saint-Exupery, a young prince learns this secret from a fox: "It is only with the heart that one sees rightly, for what is essential is invisible to the eye." What is true and what is real may be beyond what we can see. What is essential is our spiritual or inner life. This is ultimately what matters the most, since we are in reality spiritual beings occupying temporary physical bodies. **The First Pearl: Our inner life is of primary importance.**

The Second Pearl. It is not the *problems* we face but how we *approach* our problems that determines the success or failure of our efforts. Our inner world determines our approach: how we choose to interpret events and how we choose to act in response to events, regardless of the circumstances.

There is a formula that speaks to the concept of stimulus and response. It is usually assumed that a particular stimulus leads to a certain response.

$$\text{Stimulus} \longrightarrow \text{Response}$$

This is especially true with lower life forms. But many people believe it is true for human beings as well. For example, if I am insulted I have no choice but to be angry and insult back.

There is, however, another formula, which adds a variable. The next formula adds a degree of complexity indicated by the delta sign above the arrow:

$$S \overset{\triangle}{\longrightarrow} R$$

The delta sign represents a change agent that affects the formula. For humans, the change agent is our individual interpretation of a given stimulus, which affects our response.

We have this amazing freedom to interpret a stimulus (a stressor, a problem) and to then choose our response. Our response is not (or doesn't have to be) automatic. When someone insults me, before I react I can stop and consider what provoked them. It may have nothing to do with me. It may be that they are in a great deal of pain, or that their encounter with me has come after a series of unhappy encounters where they did not get the help they needed. I may remind them of someone whom they fear or regard with animosity. In other words, what they are responding to comes from the circumstances of their own life, and not from anything I have done at all. If I choose not to take it personally and respond with kindness, I may well turn their focus and the entire situation around. **The Second Pearl: Our inner life determines our approach and response to problems.**

The Third Pearl. Changing our circumstances is not the answer. Many people think they would be happy at work, in relationships, or in life, if only some circumstance (or circumstances) were different. Perhaps if the pay were better, or the hours were shorter, or they had a different boss . . . if only things on the *outside* were different. On the contrary, researchers have found that people have an innate happiness "set point." When they solve any of the issues that they felt were preventing happiness, sure enough, people feel more content and report more happiness. However, even with wonderful, life-changing events such as marriage or the birth of a child, the newfound contentment only lasts for a limited time, at most several months. Then people revert to their original levels of reported well-being.

This amazing finding is also true in relation to income levels. British economist Richard Layard writes about the "hedonic treadmill." This describes the reality that people seek higher incomes, expecting greater happiness or well-being. At each new level of income, however, their elation is short-lived, and soon they are striving for the next level.

We often hold tightly to the belief that our happiness depends on outward circumstances, but it just doesn't hold true. And this is a good thing, for otherwise we would be like lower life forms with no true freedom or power to interpret and choose our response to life. Our enthusiasm, joy, and well-being, at work or elsewhere, are utterly determined by our inner lives. It is our inner lives that determine our happiness. The inner life electrifies us, becoming the change agent or catalyst that allows us to interpret events and make choices. Now we can respond to our life situations and circumstances in an infinite number of ways.

In the inspired book *A Course in Miracles*, there is this remarkable statement: "If you knew who walked beside you at all times on this path that you have chosen, you could never experience fear again." We have a choice. We can ignore our spiritual lives and ultimately respond to our circumstances in fearful ways (by seeking more control and holding on to unmet expectations and grudges). Or by nurturing our spiritual lives, we can choose to trust in the Divine that holds us in love. This trust allows our inner lives to respond to our circumstances in ways that bring joy and fulfillment. The Third Pearl: **Our inner life and attitude determine our level of joy and happiness.**

The Fourth Pearl. In order to experience and enjoy the truth in the first three pearls, we must focus on developing a vibrant spiritual life. That is what my journey out of burnout has taught me. If the inner life is primary in importance and forms our approach and response to problems, thus determining our joy and happiness, we should want it to be at its best. So cultivate your spiritual life. Develop a daily practice that works for you, and commit to it. Feed your spirit. Watch out for complaining, holding grudges, and worrying. By learning to trust, change these habits to gratitude, forgiveness, and being at peace. Follow your calling and be of service. Let your inner life mold your attitude and fill you with peace of mind. Turn expectations and the desire to control others or situations into hope and trust in the Divine, knowing that you will be used for your best purposes. Let your spirituality frame your inner life and fill you with energy so that you may bring the best of yourself to your professional life. **The Fourth Pearl: Our inner life is at its best when we nurture our spirituality.**

These are the blessings of my journey: I traded anxiety for joy, and exhaustion for a wellspring of energy. Cynicism has been replaced by compassion. The feeling of drowning has left me, and now I feel I'm a man walking solidly upon the sacred earth. I have traded ill health for well-being, and weariness for a steady, calm flow of peace. No longer do I drag myself out of bed each day, barely able to face the morning. Now I begin the day breathing deeply of the fresh air and wondering whom I might help today. I have traded resentment for love of life.

Learning to listen to and cultivate my inner spiritual life has not only helped me to recover from burnout, it has also enabled me to bounce back and live a more balanced life. Now I bring more vitality and enthusiasm to my work. This energetic attitude affects everyone around me. It energizes my staff, and it helps and supports my patients even before we have begun treatment. This new understanding of wellness, infused with spirituality, has given me a better sense of how to read my patients. I enter each room with a prayer that stills me. I focus all my attention on the person in that moment, and my skills of observation become very acute. I am a much better doctor now, and treat my patients with a great deal more respect. My work is more fulfilling than ever before.

Every day I help people get well, care for them, and ease them a little further down their own path. In all that I do, I'm a much happier man. The only thing that has changed is my perspective, framed by a developing spirituality. I now can relate to the words of Albert Camus: "In the depth of winter, I finally learned that within me there lay an invincible summer."

Perhaps you, too, are no longer enjoying your job or profession. Maybe you once had high ideals and exciting dreams, but you now feel desperate and burned out. If so, I urge you to make a place for yourself in your life, a place in which you can hear that small inner voice. There, let yourself be soothed and healed. Let yourself listen to the quiet. Let your mind rest.

Then in days, weeks, or months—after some time has passed and you can reach that still place with ease—listen for the lessons that may apply in particular to your life. There are a myriad of spiritual traditions from which you might borrow tools. Or you may want to create your own ceremonies, your own way of approaching the Divine with reverence. Whether or not you believe in God, you are a spiritual being and all living things are linked together. Your inner Self can feel this connection and speak to you about it, offering guidance and support for your deepest concerns. Choose a practice that feels right to you, and simply begin.

Start your journey now. Take one step at a time. Be patient. Make your space. Create your ritual. Begin your journal. Then, practice remembering these moments of peace throughout the day as you relate to others. You may do this with a prayer, a meditation, or some other touchstone—whatever reminder works for you.

As you complete your wellness circle with the Four Pearls, you will watch in wonder as miracles begin to occur in your life.

Recommended Reading

Borysenko, Joan. *Fire in the Soul: A New Psychology of Spiritual Optimism*. New York: Warner Books, 1994. An inspirational guide for inner healing and moving from crisis to hope.

Carlson, Richard, and Benjamin Shield. *Handbook for the Soul*. New York: Back Bay Books, 1996. A wonderful anthology of writings by 32 renowned spiritual teachers to nurture the inner life.

Dossey, Larry. *Healing Words: The Power of Prayer and the Practice of Medicine*. San Francisco: HarperSan-Francisco, 1993. A complete and convincing presentation of the importance and place of spirituality in the practice of medicine.

Dyer, Wayne W. *Wisdom of the Ages: 60 Days to Enlightenment*. New York: Harper, 2002. A collection of writings and poems from great teachers of the past, applying their wisdom to create inner spiritual change.

Kabat-Zinn, Jon. *Wherever You Go, There You Are: Mindfulness Meditation in Everyday Life*. New York: Hyperion, 2005. A practical guide to daily meditation. Full of simple yet deep insights to improve one's practice of connecting with the inner life.

Moore, Thomas. *Care of the Soul: A Guide for Cultivating Depth and Sacredness in Everyday Life*. New York: HarperPerennial, 1994. A fascinating discussion of the soul and how nourishing the life of the spirit can address modern psychological problems.

Nhat Hanh, Thich. *Peace Is Every Step: The Path of Mindfulness in Everyday Life*. New York: Bantam Books, 1992. Inspirational and practical ideas to bring inner peace, by the famous Vietnamese Buddhist monk.

Remen, Rachel Naomi. *My Grandfather's Blessings: Stories of Strength, Refuge, and Belonging*. New York: Riverhead Books, 2000. Beautifully shared stories of practical spiritual wisdom used to bring healing.

Sluyter, Dean. *The Zen Commandments: Ten Suggestions for a Life of Inner Freedom*. New York: J.P. Tarcher/Putnam, 2001. Illuminating teachings and methods to find the joy and freedom of the inner life.

Index

To schedule a presentation with Alan Shelton, MD

please go to
www.TransformingBurnout.com

Popular topics:

1) Transforming Burnout
2) Enthusiasm and Energy at Work
3) Spirituality and the Workplace
4) Health Care Provider Wellness
5) Developing a Spiritual Practice

Alan Shelton, MD
Vibrant Press
P.O. Box 8605
Tacoma, WA 98418
(253) 627-5955